Hummingbirds

Hummingbirds

Nancy L. Newfield

KEY PORTER BOOKS

The Hummingbird Family

*I met my first hummingbird, a male Ruby-throat, in my mother's salvia
garden when I was a girl of eight or nine. Magically, he seemed to hang in the air as he
drifted from one scarlet blossom to another. His shimmering ruby gorget caught my eye. I held
my breath for fear any movement would scare him away. I blinked and he disappeared as
quickly as he had come into view. I was enchanted!*

What does it take to be a hummingbird? Most hummingbirds
are tiny birds clad in glittering iridescent feathers of many
colors—living jewels. With wing beats so rapid that they are
nearly invisible, these birds spend their days darting from flower to flower,
sipping nectar, and dazzling all who behold them. To the casual observer,
these mighty mites would seem to be insects, but they are birds in every way.

Left: A MALE
BROAD-TAILED
HUMMINGBIRD
TAKES FLIGHT.

ANCESTRY
The hummingbird family Trochilidae is most closely related to the fast-
flying, insect-eating swift family Apodidae. Members of both families have

long, narrow wings and tiny feet. Ornithologists who study hummingbirds believe that they evolved in the northern Andes of South America. But because the fragile bodies do not preserve well, there are no known fossils and much of the evolutionary history of the family is open to conjecture. Native only to the Western Hemisphere, the hummingbirds are the second largest bird family in the New World after the tyrant flycatchers. More than 320 species occur throughout the Americas from Alaska to Tierra del Fuego in southern Chile. Colombia is home to 150 or more species, while Ecuador hosts about 130. The number of species diminishes as one goes north or south from the Equator. Fifty species are known from Costa Rica in Central America while only 15 species nest in the entire United States and Canada.

The habitats to which hummingbirds have adapted are extremely diverse. The hottest, driest deserts on both continents are home to species that have evolved to wrest a living from a seemingly barren ecosystem. In the high Andes, hardy hummers build heavily felted nests and they roost in caves and crevices to conserve their energy during frigid nights. Steaming tropical rain forests, temperate woodlands, and even densely populated cities have species that have adapted to natural and man-made ecosystems.

SPECIATION

Hummer sizes vary from the 2 ½ inch (5 cm) Bee Hummingbird (*Mellisuga helenae*) of Cuba and the Isle of Pines, the tiniest bird on Earth, to almost 9 inches (22.5 cm) for the Giant Hummingbird (*Patagona gigas*) of western South America. The palette of colors that hummingbird feathers reflect is nothing short of amazing. Dozens of shades of red, blue, green, and purple array gorgets, crowns, backs, wings, and tails. And ornamentation does not stop with color. Elaborate crests, brilliant ear fans, and long flowing tails give the birds an exotic appeal. Yet, some tropical species called hermits wear somberly hued feathers streaked with green, gray, and brown.

Right:
A MEADOW ABLAZE WITH INDIAN PAINTBRUSH WILL SUPPORT MANY HUMMINGBIRDS.

SPECIES FOR NORTH AMERICA

In the vast area from the Great Plains to the Atlantic Ocean, only the Ruby-throated Hummingbird (*Archilochus colubris*) occurs during the nesting season, though several others may be found during the fall and winter. Colorful green-backed males sport sparkling red throats, called gorgets. The female's coloration is not as gaudy. Like the male, she has a shimmering emerald back, but her underparts are grayish white. Young ones resemble their mother, with males having a few red feathers showing their promise of future glory.

From central Texas westward across the Southwest to the Pacific Ocean, the Black-chinned Hummingbird (*Archilochus alexandri*) makes its home in deserts, canyons, and foothills as well as in residential gardens, where their dark green backs glow in the rays of the sun. The upper part of the male's gorget is velvety black while a band of brilliant violet feathers marks the lower edge. Otherwise, he resembles his eastern cousin. Females, too, are similar to female Ruby-throats, though the careful observer might notice a longer bill and duller gray underparts. Young birds are very similar to the female parent.

The heart of the Anna's Hummingbird (*Calypte anna*) range is California though the species has extended itself northward to British Columbia and eastward through much of southeastern Arizona. This adaptable bird is as much at ease in urban and suburban gardens as it is in coastal chaparral and mountain hideaways. The glittering rose red crown and gorget of the male stand out against his blue green back. Typical of many female hummers, the brilliant gorget and crown are lacking, except for a small spot of color in the center of the throat. Otherwise, female Anna's are green and dull gray.

In the driest deserts of southern California and Arizona, the Costa's Hummingbird (*Calypte costae*) finds the arid climate to its liking. Here, males with purple crowns and gorgets perch high atop bare snags, guarding their flowers from any intruders. Females and immatures are similar to female and immature Ruby-throated and Black-chinned Hummingbirds, with green backs and pale gray underparts.

The elegant Broad-tailed Hummingbird (*Selasphorus platycercus*) is almost symbolic of the Rocky Mountains in the West. On whistling wings, males with rosy red gorgets and shimmering bluish green backs fly amid pines and oaks at high elevations, while green-backed females with a wash of pale cinnamon on their sides slip out to meadows strewn with columbine, penstemon, and other wildflowers.

The feisty Rufous Hummingbird (*Selasphorus rufus*) lives in the mountains of the Pacific Northwest, British Columbia, and Alaska. Males with rusty-colored backs and coppery orange gorgets joust for dominance at every patch of gooseberry and currant, while their bronzy green-backed females establish nests in forests of oak and pine.

In coastal California, the closely related Allen's Hummingbird (*Selasphorus sasin*) inhabits chaparral, oak woodlands, and residential gardens. Males have green backs, but are otherwise very similar to their rusty cousins. Females and immatures are nearly identical to female and immature Rufous Hummingbirds.

The large Blue-throated Hummingbird (*Lampornis clemenciae*) enjoys moist wooded canyons in the mountains of southeastern Arizona and western Texas during the summer months. Both sexes wear bronzy green backs and have prominent white tail spots, but only the male shows the shimmering cobalt blue gorget. Immatures resemble the parent of the same sex.

Equally large is the Magnificent Hummingbird (*Eugenes fulgens*), native to the pine forests of southeastern Arizona, southwestern New Mexico, and western Texas. The spectacular male wears a fine crown of glowing purple and an emerald throat. His consort is rather plain with green upperparts and a gray throat, breast, and belly. Young males begin acquiring their

dramatically beautiful plumage soon after leaving the nest.

Also indigenous to southeastern Arizona, southwestern New Mexico, and western Texas is the Broad-billed Hummingbird (*Cynanthus latirostris)*, which frequents desert scrub and streamside cottonwoods. The colorful male is unmistakable with peacock blue underparts and a brilliant orange red bill. The green and gray female wears a blackish mask around her eyes.

The dashing Buff-bellied Hummingbird (*Amazilia yucatanensis*) inhabits brushy live oak mottes and gardens along the southern Texas coast, where the hummers find nectar in the small blossoms of hibiscuslike turk's caps. Adults and immatures of both sexes are feathered in bronzy green, with green throats and chests and pale cinnamon bellies. Females and young birds are not quite as brilliant as adult males. A slightly curved red orange bill adds a rakish touch.

The elegant Violet-crowned Hummingbird (*Amazilia violiceps*) enjoys riparian cottonwoods and sycamores in southeastern Arizona for nesting. Males and females both wear bronze-colored feathers on their backs and pristine white ones on their underparts, but only the males exhibit the characteristic glittering purple crown. The long, thick bill is vibrant orange.

The desert-dwelling Lucifer Hummingbird (*Calothorax lucifer*) lives in western Texas, southern New Mexico, and southeastern Arizona. The male's deep violet gorget has long feathers that project out from the sides. The plainer female shows underparts of pale buff. Both probe ocotillos and cactus flowers with long, decurved bills.

The White-eared Hummingbird (*Hylocharis leucotis*) is a rare visitor in southern Arizona where high elevation forests of oak and pine provide a habitat similar to that which it prefers in Mexico. The male's royal purple crown and chin contrast with a vivid red bill. The female is marked below with tiny green spots.

The Berylline Hummingbird (*Amazilia beryllina*) is found in the oak-

Left: SOFT GRAY GREEN LICHENS CAMOUFLAGE THE EXTERIOR OF THIS BROAD-TAILED HUMMINGBIRD NEST.

forested canyons of southeastern Arizona almost every summer. Males and females are similar with glittering green upperparts and throats and grayish bellies. A chestnut spot marks each wing.

From a homeland in southern Mexico, the Green Violet-ear (*Colibri thalassinus*) makes an appearance in Texas, and often other parts of North America, every year. Another rare visitor to Texas is the Green-breasted Mango (*Anthracothorax prevostii*). First discovered there in 1990, one or more is reported every year.

The region of the U.S. border with Mexico in Arizona, New Mexico, and Texas is home to a wealth of hummingbirds. And, birds do not recognize political boundaries. Occasionally, one that does not normally occur in the border region goes astray and delights the hundreds of birders who visit the Southwest. The Plain-capped Starthroat (*Heliomaster constantii*), the Cinnamon Hummingbird (*Amazilia rutila*), and the Bumblebee Hummingbird (*Atthis heloisa*) have each been recorded a few times. These vagrant birds will not likely be noticed by a casual observer. Several Xantus's Hummingbirds (*Hylocharis xantusii*) have strayed up the Pacific coast from southern Baja California and they have appeared in gardens in the U.S. and Canada.

Florida's proximity to the islands of the Caribbean also invites rare visitors. The Bahama Woodstar (*Calliphlox evelynae*) and the Cuban Emerald (*Chlorostilbon ricordii*) have been reported a few times.

LEGENDS AND MYTHS

Ancient civilizations used images of the creatures around them to symbolize forces they could not explain. The indigenous peoples of the Americas knew the hummingbird very well. Surely alluding to the hummer's bellicose nature, many a tale features a tiny, but warlike bird. Aztec legend held that slain warriors were transported to the "mansion of the sun" to become radiant hummingbirds.

RANGING AS FAR SOUTHWARD AS POSSIBLE, THE GREEN-BACKED FIRECROWN (*SEPHANOIDES SEPHANOIDES*) NESTS IN THE BLEAK, WINDSWEPT ENVIRONS OF TIERRA DEL FUEGO, CHILE.

Tribes of the southwestern states—Hopi, Zuni, and Pima—associated hummingbirds with the initiation of summer rains because the birds began nesting soon after the thunderstorm season started. To molest a nest might cause disastrous flooding. Navajos admired the hummingbird's valor and placed it with the eagle and wolf as a symbol of courage.

In the Pacific Northwest, the spring arrival of the hummingbird was associated with good luck and fair weather by the 'Ksan people. This tribe related the new crop of salmonberries to pollination by the birds.

This Green Mango (*Anthracothorax viridis*)
remains alert for danger in a Puerto Rican thicket.

THIS VIOLET-
CROWNED
WOODNYMPH
(*THALURANIA
COLOMBICA*)
INHABITS TROP-
ICAL LOWLAND
FORESTS FROM
GUATEMALA TO
COLOMBIA AND
VENEZUELA.

PREENING REMOVES MITES AND KEEPS FEATHERS IN GOOD CONDITION.

A FEMALE BROAD-TAILED HUMMINGBIRD INCUBATES CLOSELY.

FROM HIS PERCH LOW IN A TROPICAL DRY FOREST
IN COSTA RICA, A CINNAMON HUMMINGBIRD (*AMAZILIA RUTILA*)
WAITS FOR A PASSING BUG.

THE DARK BEAUTY OF THIS MALE MAGNIFICENT HUMMINGBIRD
EARNS HIM THE NICKNAME "BLACK KNIGHT."

The Purple-throated Mountain-gem (*Lampornis calolaema*) is widespread in the highlands from Nicaragua to Panama.

THE CUBAN EMERALD IS COMMON IN THE FORESTS
OF THE BAHAMAS AND CUBA.

Above: LIMITED TO A SINGLE CARIBBEAN ISLAND, THE
PUERTO RICAN EMERALD (*CHLOROSTILBON MAUGAEUS*) INHABITS
WOODLANDS FROM SEA LEVEL TO HIGH MOUNTAINS.

Right: A MALE BLUE-THROATED HUMMINGBIRD SHOWS HIS
SOMBER, MOUSE GRAY BREAST AND BELLY.

Above: A VIBRANT RED BILL AND PRISTINE WHITE
UNDERPARTS SET THE VIOLET-CROWNED HUMMINGBIRD APART
FROM OTHER MEMBERS OF ITS FAMILY.

Left: AN IMMATURE MALE RUFOUS HUMMINGBIRD STANDS
GUARD OVER HIS TERRITORY.

The Hummingbird Family

HUMMINGBIRDS

Above: THE PURPLE GORGET AND CROWN OF THE
MALE COSTA'S HUMMINGBIRD GLISTEN IN THE SCORCHING SUN
OF WESTERN DESERTS.

Left: IN A REMOTE DESERT HABITAT, THIS LUCIFER HUMMINGBIRD
FACES FEW THREATS FROM RAMPANT REAL ESTATE DEVELOPMENT.

A MALE WINE-THROATED HUMMINGBIRD (*ATTHIS ELLIOTI*) ON THE
LEFT FLARES HIS GORGET TO IMPRESS A PROSPECTIVE MATE.

FREQUENT GROOMING REMOVES EXTERNAL PARASITES
AND WORN FEATHERS.

HUMMINGBIRDS

Above: The long, extensile gorget feathers of the male Calliope Hummingbird are unique among North American hummers.

Left: The unique Juan Fernandez Firecrown (*Sephanoides fernandensis*) is the most endangered hummingbird on Earth. The entire range of the species is the tiny Isla Robinson Crusoe, which is located 350 miles (560 km) off the coast of Chile. The female is colored so differently that she might not be recognizable as the same species.

Above: THE GREEN VIOLET-EAR MOVES NORTH FROM ITS
RANGE IN SOUTHERN MEXICO TO APPEAR IN TEXAS AND OTHER
STATES EVERY YEAR.

Right: WITH A UNIQUE COLOR PATTERN, THIS TINY SNOWCAP
(*MICROCHERA ALBOCORONATA*) IS HIGHLY SOUGHT IN ITS EASTERN
CENTRAL AMERICAN HAUNTS.

The Hummer Lifestyle

To be successful in a biological sense, each creature must reproduce itself. That means that every female has to produce two young that survive long enough to reproduce. It would seem easy for a single hummingbird to accomplish this goal, but these are birds that live on the edge. Mortality in the first year exacts a terrible price. Still, there doesn't seem to be any shortage of hummers. I know no greater thrill than to find a nest where I can observe the next generation prepare to challenge destiny.

TERRITORIES

Left: SECLUDED WITHIN A DESERT SHRUB, THIS FEMALE COSTA'S HUMMINGBIRD TENDS HER TWO CHICKS.

The territory is the nucleus of a hummingbird's world, aggressively defended by intimidation and by vocalizations. Each male maintains an exclusive area for feeding and breeding females protect their nests. A territory might be held for only a few minutes while a hummer feeds at a certain patch of flowers during migration or it might be maintained for several months if the blossoms remain prolific. The most powerful bird in any area will usually hold the most productive territory.

DISPLAYS

To assert territorial claims during the breeding season and to attract and impress potential mates, male hummingbirds put on dramatic, stylized displays. With powerful dives, the bird traces a huge "J" or "U" or "O" in the air. One particular shape is distinctive for each species. These power dives are often accompanied by vocalizations and sounds produced by wind passing through the wing or tail feathers. Intruding males usually flee at the onslaught, but physical combat is sometimes necessary.

COURTSHIP AND NESTING

When a seemingly receptive female enters a male's territory, his excitement grows. He moves closer and presses his suit more strongly by flying an intimate side-to-side display called a shuttle. A receptive female will remain perched for several minutes before flying away. The male pursues the female and mating takes place away from his territory.

During copulation, the female perches on a low twig, while the male mounts her back. Very quickly, he dips his tail so that his vent touches the female's vent, permitting transfer of the sperm. After mating, the two fly off in different directions.

Males take no part in nest-building, incubation, or care of the young. Their role is limited to fertilization of the female's eggs. The pair bond that is so important to many songbirds does not exist for hummingbirds, but nonetheless males often permit females to feed within their territories.

The female hummer selects a nest site and initiates construction before she begins to look for a mate. Preferred sites vary from one species to another though many prefer a slender downward-curving branch. Others may opt for a cactus, an electrical wire, or other man-made object. Often overhanging leaves obscure the nest.

Generally, the nest is built of plant down and bits of leaves and grass. It is

Right:
COLORFUL CHUPAROSAS DOT A HILL-SIDE WHERE HUMMERS ABOUND.

Above: A FEMALE MAGNIFICENT HUMMINGBIRD APPROACHES A
FEEDER TO TAKE ADVANTAGE OF THE FREE MEAL.

Left: THE LARGE MAGNIFICENT HUMMINGBIRD CAN EASILY
DOMINATE ALL THE FOOD SOURCES IN AN AREA.

held together and saddled to the site by spider webs. Tiny pieces of lichen
disguise the outside, making it appear to be part of the twig. The finished
nest is about the size of half a walnut shell. In arid climates, fragments of
dried flowers are sometimes substituted for the lichens. The nest must be
warm and durable, yet it must dry quickly.

The female seeks the male in his territory. After mating, she returns to her nest. She lays two white eggs two days apart. The navy bean-sized eggs are incubated for about 15 days, beginning with the laying of the second egg. During incubation, the female hummer leaves only to eat and to chase intruders, which might include her mate.

YOUNG

Naked, blind, and helpless, the newly hatched hummer might seem ugly to the human eye. It is the size of a honey bee, with a mere stub for a bill. Fed by regurgitation on a high-protein diet of insects and nectar collected by the female, the nestlings grow quickly. The female inserts her long, needlelike bill into the throat of a young one and literally pumps nourishment into it. If sufficient food is unavailable near the nest, she may travel a mile (1.6 km) or more to a reliable source.

When the young are newly hatched, they are unable to control their own body temperature, so the female warms them with her body and shelters them from the elements. As they develop and grow feathers, the nestlings need less brooding. At the same time, their rapid growth requires the female to find an ever-increasing amount of food for her youngsters—and herself!

By the time the nestlings are 21-25 days old, they are fully feathered and nearly the size of their parents. As time for fledging approaches, the youngsters exercise their wings and move about the nest, which stretches to near bursting. Indeed, a poorly constructed nest may split apart, spilling still helpless nestlings to the ground before they are ready to fly. There, they will succumb to exposure or predators.

To practice for flying, nearly grown nestlings exercise their wings while still holding onto the bottom of the nest with their feet. After a few days, the youngsters gain some confidence and let go. A hummer's first flight is far from graceful. The young bird often flies only a few feet. Then it crash lands onto a nearby twig. It takes a few days and a lot of practice before they develop the mastery of the air for which hummingbirds are famous. The mother continues to feed her young during their first few days of freedom, but as soon as they are capable of feeding themselves, she chases her progeny away.

Adult hummers do not have many predators, but hawks, snakes, praying mantises and large spiders can catch some. Young in the nest are vulnerable to snakes, squirrels, and birds such as jays. Still, many birds are overconfident of their ability to escape danger. House cats and other predators claim those that wait too long to flee.

FEATHERS AND MOLT

Feathers set birds apart from all other creatures. They provide the bird with lightweight protection from the elements. Wing and tail feathers enable flight and facilitate maneuverability.

Brilliant iridescent feathers give hummers their sparkle. Microscopic flat bubbles within the matrix of the feather refract light, creating the glitter and the illusion of various colors. A single feather might appear to be green, gold, orange, or red, depending on the angle from which the light is coming.

In addition to their ordinary feathers, some hummers have fascinating ornamentation. Coquettes of the genus *Lophornis* sport spiky crests and gorgets with long projecting feathers on the side. Members of the genus *Colibri* are called violet-ears for their extensible glittering purple ear fans. Long, flowing tails of the sylphs *Aglaiocercus* of northern South America shimmer violet or turquoise in the tropical sun. The male Marvelous Spatule-tail (*Loddigesia mirabilis*) uses two iridescent disks at the end of long, wirelike shafts in its tail like semaphores during displays to females. It lives only in the isolated Utcubamba Valley in northern Peru. The wing and tail feathers of the Rufous, Allen's, and Broad-tailed are highly modified to produce non-vocal sounds during regular flight and courtship displays.

A FEMALE BROAD-BILLED HUMMINGBIRD PICKS UP A LOAD
OF POLLEN WHILE SATSIFYING HER HUNGER.

Two well-fed fledglings snooze while waiting for their next meal.

Above: ANNA'S HUMMINGBIRDS ARE A FAMILIAR GARDEN
BIRD IN CALIFORNIA AND ARIZONA.

Right: THE DEEP CUP-SHAPED NEST OF THE RUBY-THROATED
HUMMINGBIRD ENSURES THE SAFETY OF THE PRECIOUS EGGS.

Above: DESERT LOBELIA HOLDS A MEAL FOR THIS BROAD-BILLED
HUMMINGBIRD.

Left: MANY FEMALE HUMMERS, LIKE THIS
VIOLET-CROWNED WOODNYMPH WEAR LESS GAUDY COLORS THAN
THEIR MALE COUNTERPARTS. QUIET HUES MAKE THEM LESS
NOTICEABLE TO PREDATORS.

Above: THIS RUBY-THROATED HUMMINGBIRD'S GORGET MIRRORS
THE SCARLET HUES OF HIS FAVORITE BERGAMOT FLOWERS.

Left: THE RUFOUS HUMMINGBIRD IS ONE OF THE MOST
AGGRESSIVE IN ITS FEISTY FAMILY.

Above: THE STREAMERTAIL (*TROCHILUS POLYTMUS*) HAS
BEEN NICKNAMED "DOCTORBIRD" BY JAMAICANS, WHO RECOGNIZE
IT AS THEIR NATIONAL BIRD.

Left: A FEMALE BROAD-BILLED HUMMINGBIRD PREPARES TO PUMP
NOURISHMENT INTO HER SINGLE CHICK.

Above: A SOFT FEATHER WILL ADD CUSHIONING TO THE
INSIDE OF THE NEST.

Left: AN OCOTILLO FLOWERS IN THE RUGGED DESERT OF THE
ORGAN PIPE CACTUS NATIONAL MONUMENT IN ARIZONA.

Above: FLASHING HIS DEEP SAPPHIRE GORGET,
THIS MALE BLUE-THROATED HUMMINGBIRD SEEMS READY TO
CHASE ANY INTERLOPERS.

Right: WITH CRIMSON GORGET AGLOW, THIS MALE
RUBY-THROATED HUMMINGBIRD WATCHES FOR FEMALES WITH
WHICH TO MATE.

A TINY MALE CALLIOPE HUMMINGBIRD PERCHES
QUIETLY BETWEEN FEEDING FORAYS.

An Azure-crowned Hummingbird (*Amazilia cyanocephala*) pollinates a Mexican gesneriad.

Above: THE NEWLY HATCHED HUMMINGBIRD HAS A LONG WAY
TO GO BEFORE IT BECOMES A FLYING JEWEL.

Left: A MALE RUFOUS HUMMINGBIRD INVESTIGATES
FAIRY DUSTER FLOWERS.

Above: THE EXTRA LONG BILL OF THE LUCIFER HUMMINGBIRD
ENABLES HIM TO REACH DEEP INTO FLOWERS TO HARVEST THEIR
SWEET NECTAR.

Right: THE PURPLE-GORGETED LUCIFER
HUMMINGBIRD LIVES ONLY IN A FEW REMOTE DESERTS IN THE
UNITED STATES AND MEXICO.

Flight and Migration

The ability of birds to transport themselves is truly incredible.
When I think of the geography a single bird might cover, I am filled with
admiration. The Rufous Hummingbird I see sipping nectar from the orange, bell-shaped
blossoms of the flowering maple has come from Oregon, Washington, British Columbia, or
Alaska—places I'll likely never see. On his own power, he has moved from the towering
Pacific Northwestern rain forests to the rugged peaks of the Sierra Nevadas to the
vast Sonoran desert. Maybe he's come eastward across the juniper-clad hill
country of central Texas; maybe he's seen the Sierra Madres in Mexico.
And, he makes this journey twice a year! Awesome!

Left: A LARGE STAND OF PENSTEMON MAKES A SPLASH OF COLOR AT THE McGILL CAMPGROUND ON MOUNT PINOS IN CALIFORNIA.

MECHANICS OF FLIGHT

Hummingbirds are as remarkable for their fast and agile flight as they are for their brilliant plumage. No other bird can fly forward, backward, in place, and upside down! Flight is a marvelous adaptation that enables birds to escape from predators, secure food from difficult to reach places, and travel long distances.

Hummer wings appear to be small for the size of the bird, but powerful breast muscles, which make up a substantial portion of a hummer's mass, drive the wings. They are capable of being rotated 180 degrees, enabling the bird to gain lift on the upstroke as well as on the downstroke. At a rate of 50-80 beats per second, the wing motion is too rapid to be captured by the human eye. Motion picture photography was originally used to study hummingbird flight in the 1960s.

Ordinary forward flight can be as fast as 30 miles (48 km) per hour, though it often seems more rapid. Power dives during displays may reach 60 miles (96 km) per hour. To hover, the bird moves its wings in a figure-eight fashion, much as a swimmer might tread water. Backward and upside down flight are only used for short distances, primarily to escape predators.

Hovering is an adaptation that enables hummingbirds to secure nectar from delicate blossoms without having to perch. In that way, they can successfully compete with most insects, which must land on the flower to reach the sweet fluid. Other kinds of birds have the ability to hover, but none does it as skillfully as the hummingbird.

MIGRATION

The majority of North American hummingbirds move away from their breeding areas after nesting chores are done. Mexico is the main destination for most, though the eastern-breeding Ruby-throat often goes as far south as central Costa Rica. The urge to migrate is triggered by hormonal changes brought about by changes in the length of daylight hours, but not all hummingbirds migrate according to the same schedule.

Migration is an adaptation that permits birds to nest in an area that has abundant food for only part of the year. The natural cycles of food availability vary from one region of the continent to another. Winter rain and a frost-free climate on the West Coast ensures an adequate supply of

Left: A MALE ANNA'S HUMMINGBIRD ORIENTS HIMSELF SO THAT SUNLIGHT REFLECTS FROM HIS GORGET AND CROWN.

nectar and insects, making the months of December, January, and February optimal for several California natives—Allen's Hummingbird, Costa's Hummingbird, and Anna's Hummingbird—some of which vacate nesting areas at other times of the year.

The colder sections of North America cannot support nectar-eating birds during the winter months, so hummers there must depart in late summer. Hummingbirds do not wait until food supplies are depleted to initiate their movements, but rather time their migrations to coincide with maximum wildflower blooms along the route. One ornithologist who studied southward migrating Rufous Hummingbirds found that individuals continued to move until they depleted most of their stored fat. Then, they ate heartily, packing on new fat for a few days, after which they continued their journey.

Most western species follow a Pacific coastal route in their northward movement from Mexico. The flight southward after nesting seems to follow mountain ridges and river valleys. Migration of Ruby-throats in the East has not been well studied. In the spring, many courageously set out northward across the Gulf of Mexico from the Yucatan Peninsula, while others travel up the coast of Texas. But after nesting, the majority move southward along the western edge of the Gulf of Mexico in late summer.

Right: GARDENS DESIGNED TO ATTRACT HUMMINGBIRDS LIKE THIS ONE IN HIGH ISLAND, TEXAS, ARE INCREASINGLY POPULAR.

Above: A Costa's Hummingbird perches near its food supply.

Right: A young Costa's Hummingbird learns to find its own nectar from desert honeysuckle.

Above: A FEMALE COSTA'S HUMMINGBIRD PREPARES TO FEED
HER DEMANDING CHICK.

Left: BILL DUSTED WITH POLLEN, THIS MALE COSTA'S
HUMMINGBIRD MOVES TO THE NEXT BLOSSOM.

Above: NEWLY FLEDGED NEST MATES REMAIN TOGETHER
FOR A FEW DAYS.

Right: A FEMALE HUMMER DISPLAYS HER WHITE
TAIL SPOTS. ORNITHOLOGISTS BELIEVE THE SPOTS ARE USED
TO INTIMIDATE INTRUDERS.

Above: A FEMALE COSTA'S HUMMINGBIRD STAYS WITH HER CHICKS
FOR A FEW WEEKS AFTER THEY HAVE LEFT THE NEST.

Left: A FEMALE COSTA'S HUMMINGBIRD FINDS NECTAR IN THE
TUBULAR, RED BLOSSOM OF A PENSTEMON.

Above: HUMMINGBIRDS CLEAN THEIR BILLS AFTER
EATING NECTAR BECAUSE THE STICKY SYRUP CAN SEAL THE BILL
CLOSED AS IT DRIES.

Right: THE BLACK-CHINNED HUMMINGBIRD LIVES AS EASILY IN
SUBURBAN GARDENS AS IN SOUTHWESTERN DESERTS.

Above: An Indian paintbrush satisfies the hunger of a White-eared Hummingbird.

Left: A female Broad-billed Hummingbird takes man-made nectar from a feeder.

Above: The purple band below the velvety black
gorget of the male Black-chinned Hummingbird is unique
among North American hummers.

Right: A male Ruby-throated Hummingbird approaches a
cluster of bergamot flowers.

Above: LARGE WHITE TAIL SPOTS ENABLE THIS BLUE-THROATED
HUMMINGBIRD TO APPEAR LARGER THAN HE IS.

Right: A FEMALE RUFOUS HUMMINGBIRD EXPLORES FOR FOOD.

Flight and Migration

Above: A FEMALE BLACK-CHINNED HUMMINGBIRD CHASES A MALE
RUFOUS HUMMINGBIRD FROM HER FEEDER.

Left: BATHING IS AN IMPORTANT PART OF EVERY
HUMMER'S DAILY ROUTINE. THIS BLUE-THROATED HUMMINGBIRD
HAS FOUND A SWIFT STREAM. HE ALWAYS PREENS CAREFULLY
AFTER HIS SPLASHING.

Above: A Green Violet-ear engages in its daily grooming.

Left: The large, powerful Blue-throated Hummingbird dominates smaller hummers throughout its range.

Ecology

*One of life's simplest pleasures is to watch hummers going
about their daily lives. I love to go afield in spring and watch the females gather
nesting materials. I treasure the memories of males displaying ardently above their
patches of wildflowers. Observing the flood of youngsters learning to find their own food
completes part of the cycle. I rejoice to see the ones I know from home on their
wintering grounds far south of the border and know that they
have safely found their way.*

FOODS

Nectar from flowers is the primary food that fuels the high-energy lifestyle of all hummingbirds. Nectar varies in concentration from about 12 percent sugar to about 50 percent sugar. Hummingbirds prefer the more dilute nectars while bees and other insects like the stronger concentrations. Typical hummingbird flowers are those that are red, orange, or pink, though flowers in other colors also produce nectar and are visited by the birds. Those flowers with a long tubular shape often

Left: HUMMERS CHECK OUT EVERYTHING RED TO SEE IF IT WILL YIELD NECTAR.

Above: THE BLUE-THROATED HUMMINGBIRD IS ONE OF THE
LARGEST MEMBERS OF ITS FAMILY IN THE UNITED STATES.

Right: A MALE BROAD-BILLED HUMMINGBIRD IN PERFECT PLUMAGE
WAITS TO DIGEST HIS LAST MEAL.

exclude bees and other insects, which compete with hummingbirds for the
sweet, sticky food. Hummingbirds have little sense of smell, so as a rule, the
flowers hummingbirds visit have no fragrance.

At times when weather is cold and food scarce, hummingbirds can slow
their metabolism to conserve energy by becoming torpid. During torpor, the
bird can appear to be dead, and it does not rouse easily. Body functions are
so greatly diminished that fewer calories are needed to sustain life.

Columbine, larkspur, and penstemon are favorites in the Rocky Mountains while jewelweed, bee balm, and cardinal flower entice hummers in the East and Midwest. In the swamps and woodlands of the Deep South, trumpet creeper and cross vine are powerful attractants. Pollen from a flower sticks to the bird's crown, throat, chest, or bill and is deposited on the next flower the bird visits. In this way, hummingbirds fertilize many blossoms while finding their daily sustenance. Throughout North America, hundreds of native plants have evolved along with the birds.

Minute flying insects and tiny spiders make up a small, but vital, part of the hummingbird's diet. Sallying forth into a cloud of nearly invisible gnats, a hummer may snatch dozens of little bugs to secure the protein, vitamins, and minerals that are essential for growth and cell repair. Spiders are often gleaned from the undersides of leaves. Females triple the amount of protein foods they consume while they are raising young.

Sap from trees and other plant fluids are similar in composition to nectar. Hummingbirds are known to consume sap, especially at times when nectar might be scarce. They also eat pollen during their floral forays, but scientists believe that the pollen is not digested.

Left: THE VIOLET-CROWNED HUMMINGBIRD ENJOYS THE SECLUSION OF SYCAMORE AND COTTONWOOD STREAM EGDES ALONG THE UNITED STATES BORDER WITH MEXICO.

HABITATS

Hummingbirds make their homes in a wide assortment of ecosystems around the continent. Almost every type of habitat in North America supports one or more species. Only Arctic tundra and ice-clad mountaintops are hummerless. Major requirements for hummingbirds are no different than the necessities for other types of birds—food, water, cover, and nesting sites.

The wide-ranging Ruby-throated Hummingbird seeks pine and oak woodlands, cypress swamps, pasture edges, parks, and gardens. Its western counterpart, the Black-chinned Hummingbird, is found in more arid regions, but often frequents open oak woodlands, orchards, damp gullies, arid foothills, and deserts. Broad-tailed Hummingbirds require mountainous woodlands and meadows carpeted with wildflowers.

The tiny Calliope Hummingbird enjoys mountain meadows and thickets of willow and alder, while the Costa's Hummingbird finds its nectar in cactus blossoms and ephemeral wildflowers in the hottest, driest deserts. Rufous Hummingbirds haunt the edges of coniferous forests, going out into adjacent fields to forage.

While both the Anna's and Allen's Hummingbirds explore brushy chaparral and oak woodlands, they are adaptable enough to be able to coexist among human developments. Exotic gardens with trees and shrubs from Asia, Africa, and Australia supplant native vegetation in many places, yet these birds learn to extract nectar from blossoms designed to accommodate other animals.

In the Southwest where lofty mountains emerge from seemingly unpromising wasteland, several species seek different niches within a particular geographical area, thus allowing each to find its specific foods and nesting sites without competing for limited resources. Within the wide range of elevations, Broad-billed and Violet-crowned Hummingbirds take lower, scrubby territories, leaving more verdant, cooler sites to Magnificent and Blue-throated Hummingbirds. In isolated places, Lucifer Hummingbirds share resources with Black-chinned Hummingbirds by making their nests on stalks of agaves and other barren-country plants.

The brush country of southern Texas is sparsely populated, leaving much of the native habitat of grasslands interspersed with dense stands of live oaks intact. Sheltered by trees, flowers are able to withstand a withering subtropical sun. Buff-bellied Hummingbirds enjoy the isolation and ready supply of nectar and insects that ensure nesting success.

GARDENS AND FEEDERS

Since nectar-rich blossoms provide a large part of the hummingbird's food, gardens are a wonderful place to look for hummers. Throughout the United States and Canada, public and private gardens designed with the hummer in mind create oases amid the sprawl of urban life. But any homeowner can enjoy these birds by turning their own yard into a haven for hummers. Carefully selected shrubs and perennials add beauty and invite passing hummers to drop in and visit. Bright red feeders dispense an inexhaustible supply of sweet sugar water. Fountains, birdbaths, and misters encourage bathing. Create the habitat and hummingbirds will come!

Hummingbirds can be lured into returning time after time by providing artificial nectar made of 1 part cane sugar to 4 parts boiling water. Allow the solution to cool before pouring it into a feeder. Red coloring, vitamins, minerals, and protein need not be added as the simple syrup in the feeder is merely a supplement to the natural foods the birds find for themselves. Feeders should be changed every few days and they must be kept clean by soaking in a hot bath of water and chlorine bleach.

Hummingbird attracting is now a large business. Lodges and restaurants that cater to nature tourists lure guests with the promise of a close encounter. Nurseries often feature displays of plants known to attract hummers and there are numerous books that instruct the homeowner on how to entice the birds. Shops and catalogues now offer a vast array of feeders and hummer gifts. Several ecotour companies design itineraries to maximize the number of different hummingbirds their clients see.

The large, powerful Violet Sabrewing
(*Campylopterus hemileucurus*) dominates feeders near the
Monteverde Cloud Forest Reserve in Costa Rica.

VARIATIONS IN THE ANGLE FROM WHICH LIGHT
STRIKES THIS VIOLET-CROWNED WOODNYMPH CREATE THE
IMPRESSION OF A CHANGE OF COLOR.

Above: THE MOUNTAINS OF COSTA RICA AND PANAMA FORM THE ENTIRE
RANGE OF THE WHITE-THROATED MOUNTAIN-GEM (*LAMPORNIS CASTANEOVENTRIS*). THIS ONE IS
SEARCHING FOR MINUTE INSECTS.

Right: THE BOLD AND AGGRESSIVE BUFF-BELLIED HUMMINGBIRD OFTEN PERCHES IN A
SECLUDED SPOT TO GUARD ITS FEEDING TERRITORY.

Above: ALBINISM IS A COMPLETE LACK OF PIGMENTATION
OF THE FEATHERS AND THE BILL, FEET, AND EYES. BIRDS THAT
WEAR WHITE PLUMAGE BUT HAVE A NORMAL DARK EYE, BILL,
AND FEET ARE REFERRED TO AS LEUCISTIC. THIS LEUCISTIC
RUBY-THROATED HUMMINGBIRD IS A YOUNG FEMALE.

Left: TROPICAL EVERGREEN FORESTS FROM COSTA
RICA TO ECUADOR ARE HOME TO THE LARGE GREEN-CROWNED
BRILLIANT (*HELIODOXA JACULA*).

Above: Grayish edges to the feathers of his
crown and a single colored gorget feather mark this
Ruby-throated Hummingbird as a young male.

Right: A male Ruby-throated Hummingbird displays
his finest colors.

Above: A YOUNG RUBY-THROATED HUMMINGBIRD
INVESTIGATES THE RED PETALS OF A CANNA LILY. HUMMERS
LEARN BY TRIAL AND ERROR.

Left: HUMMERS QUICKLY LEARN THAT FEEDERS
PROVIDE AN EASY MEAL.

Above: A MOLTING MALE BROAD-TAILED HUMMINGBIRD
SPLASHES IN A SPRAY OF WATER.

Left: AN UNDERSTORY OF RHODODENDRONS MAKES THIS
REDWOOD FOREST AN ATTRACTIVE HUMMINGBIRD HABITAT.

Above: THE VIOLET SABREWING HAUNTS TROPICAL FORESTS AND
EDGES FROM SOUTHERN MEXICO TO WESTERN PANAMA.

Right: HUMMERS ENJOY DAILY GROOMING. THIS
MALE BROAD-BILLED HUMMINGBIRD KEEPS UP HIS HANDSOME
APPEARANCE.

Above: POWDERPUFF IS WIDELY GROWN IN FROST-FREE AREAS OF
CALIFORNIA TO ATTRACT HUMMERS.

Right: THE ROCKY MOUNTAINS ARE HOME TO THE ELEGANT
BROAD-TAILED HUMMINGBIRD.

Above: A FEMALE COSTA'S HUMMINGBIRD ENJOYS A QUIET
MEAL AFTER RAISING HER YOUNG.

Left: YOUNG HUMMERS ARE ALWAYS HUNGRY. THIS
FEMALE RUBY-THROATED HUMMINGBIRD WORKS HARD TO KEEP
HER YOUNGSTERS FULL.

HUMMINGBIRDS

Above: A MALE RUFOUS HUMMINGBIRD REFRESHES HIMSELF
IN A COOL STREAM.

Left: NECTAR FROM DESERT LOBELIA WILL GIVE THIS MALE
LUCIFER HUMMINGBIRD A BURST OF ENERGY.

Communication

*Fortified with a cup of strong coffee, I step out onto the deck every
morning, listening for the golden sounds of early morning. My ears fill with the
reverie of songbirds tuning up for another day. I listen most intently for the soft 'tchew'
of the first Ruby-throat. I'm not an early riser by nature, but it is worth a little lost sleep to
be able to enjoy their voices without the discordant clatter of urban life. Few people
appreciate the 'chp' of the Rufous, the 'chrp' of the Broad-tailed, the 'ch-cht'
of the Buff-bellied. Hummer repertoires are truly amazing!*

VOCALIZATIONS

Of North American trochilids, only a few, especially the Anna's
Hummingbird, sing as part of their courtship ritual. Though
they are not well known as songsters, all produce a considerable
number of vocal sounds to communicate with each other and with other
creatures. Members of each species give distinctive chips and chatters to
announce their presence and to assert territorial claims. Hummingbird
vocalizations have not been studied as intensively as those of many

Above: STRIPS OF BARK AND GRASSES COVER THE OUTSIDE OF THIS
BROAD-BILLED HUMMINGBIRD'S NEST.

Left: FEMALE HUMMINGBIRDS CONTINUE FEEDING THEIR YOUNG
FOR A WEEK OR SO AFTER THE YOUNGSTERS FLEDGE.

songbirds, yet the observer intent on learning more about these little birds
will profit from focusing attention on the various sounds.

Among Central and South American hummingbirds, several are skilled
singers. Members of a dull-colored group called hermits and other species
that lack the vibrant plumage of their kin, form singing groups called leks

where males rely on songs to vie for the attentions of neighborhood females. Several authorities have commented that the Wedge-billed Hummingbird (*Schistes geoffroyi*) of northern South America is a fine singer, but its single sweet note cannot compare with the song of the Wedge-tailed Sabrewing (*Campylopterus curvipennis*) of Mexico and northern Central America. The sabrewing's song is complex with wrenlike trills and cascades that are very pleasing to the human ear.

Right: A BUFF-BELLIED HUMMINGBIRD RAISES TWO YOUNGSTERS IN A LUSH TROPICAL GARDEN.

BODY LANGUAGE

In addition to their vocalizations, hummers use display flights and postures to communicate to other hummingbirds. The stylized displays express territoriality and breeding readiness, important components of the hummingbird lifestyle. Another approach used by both males and females to intimidate interlopers is for the territory owner to fly up to the intruder and hover with spread tail, creating an illusion of being larger. The white tail spots of the female give her an edge as they add to the effect. Perched birds sometimes use a similar technique. They puff their feathers and stretch their necks creating the impression of being larger and heavier than they are.

In Ecuador, female Booted Racket-tails (*Ocreatus underwoodii*) often throw their heads back and emit a musical whinny when encountering other hummers. The purpose of this action is not clear, but it may be to warn intruders that they are too close for comfort.

CONCLUSION

Many people think of hummingbirds as fragile creatures because of their diminutive size and sparkling colors, but they are as remarkable for their toughness and resilience as for their gem-like qualities. They add glamour to a desert landscape and wildness to a suburban garden. What remarkable versatility for a creature that weighs little more than a dime!

Above: A MALE RUBY-THROATED HUMMINGBIRD EXPLORES THE
PINK FLOWERS OF A PENTAS.

Left: PURPLE FEATHERS ON THE LOWER GORGET OF THE
BLACK-CHINNED HUMMINGBIRD APPEAR BLACK UNLESS LIGHT
STRIKES FROM DIRECTLY BEHIND THE OBSERVER.

Above: IMMATURE MALE RUFOUS HUMMINGBIRDS ARE
INDISTINGUISHABLE FROM ALLEN'S HUMMINGBIRDS OF THE SAME AGE AND SEX.

Left: THE SLOPES OF LASSEN PEAK IN NORTHERN
CALIFORNIA ARE A FERTILE NESTING GROUND FOR BROAD-TAILED
AND CALLIOPE HUMMINGBIRDS.

HUMMINGBIRDS

Above: YOUNG COSTA'S HUMMINGBIRDS EXERCISE THEIR WINGS
BEFORE TRYING TO FLY.

Left: LOOSE FEATHERS ARE PULLED OUT WHEN HUMMINGBIRDS
GROOM THEMSELVES.

Above: A HEAVY COATING OF POLLEN ON THE CROWN AND
BILL OF THIS FEMALE COSTA'S HUMMINGBIRD INDICATES SHE HAS
BEEN HARD AT WORK FINDING NECTAR FOR HER CHICKS.

Left: THE BUFF-BELLIED HUMMINGBIRD INHABITS BRUSH LANDS
AND GARDENS ALONG THE LOWER TEXAS COAST.

Above: A NEWLY FLEDGED ANNA'S HUMMINGBIRD MUST QUICKLY
LEARN TO FIND ITS OWN FOOD.

Right: HUMMERS SEARCH FOR TINY INSECTS AS WELL
AS NECTAR. THIS BROAD-BILLED HUMMINGBIRD SEEMS TO BE
INSPECTING THE PLANT'S STEMS.

Above: A Rufous Hummingbird goes through his
morning exercises.

Left: Old and worn feathers are replaced at least once
each year in a process called molt.

TWO READY-TO-FLEDGE BROAD-TAILED HUMMINGBIRDS FILL
THEIR NEST TO NEAR BURSTING.

Adding a feather to her nest, this Costa's Hummingbird
prepares for a few hectic weeks of motherhood.

Sugar from nectar powers the high energy
hummingbird lifestyle.

Hummingbirds

THIS POLLEN-DUSTED CALLIOPE HUMMINGBIRD
ENSURES THAT THE ROCKY MOUNTAIN BEEPLANT WILL PRODUCE
A HEALTHY SUPPLY OF SEED.

TWO EGGS ARE A COMPLETE CLUTCH FOR ALL SPECIES OF
HUMMINGBIRDS.

YELLOW POLLEN OBSCURES THE GLITTERING FUCHSIA-COLORED
CROWN OF THIS ANNA'S HUMMINGBIRD.

EACH FLOWER PROVIDES A SMALL DROP OF NECTAR. EVERY BIRD
MUST VISIT MANY BLOSSOMS OVER THE COURSE OF A DAY.

References

American Ornithologists' Union. 1998. *Check-list of North American Birds*. 7th ed. Washington, D.C.

Johnsgard, Paul A. 1983. *Hummingbirds of North America*. Washington, D. C.: Smithsonian Institution Press.

Newfield, Nancy L. and Barbara Nielsen. 1996. *Hummingbird Gardens: Attracting Nature's Jewels to Your Backyard*. Boston: Houghton Mifflin Co.

Skutch, Alexander F. 1973. *The Life of the Hummingbird*. New York: Crown Publishers.

Toops, Connie. 1992. *Hummingbirds: Jewels in Flight*. Stillwater, Minnesota: Voyageur Press.

Tyrrell, Esther Q. 1985. *Hummingbirds: Their Life and Behavior*. New York: Crown Publishers.